When Love is Not Enough

Parenting a Child with Trauma, Reactive Attachment Disorder, and Borderline Traits

When Love is Not Enough

Parenting a Child with Trauma, Reactive Attachment Disorder, and Borderline Traits

RJ Koehler

© 2025 RJ Koehler

All rights reserved. No part of this book may be reproduced, stored in a retrieval system, or transmitted in any form or by any means—electronic, mechanical, photocopying, recording, or otherwise—without the prior written permission of the author, except for brief quotations used in reviews or scholarly works.

This book is a work of nonfiction/memoir. Names, characters, and incidents are used with discretion to protect privacy.

Copyright registered with the U.S. Copyright Office.

Self-published in Northern Pennsylvania, United States.

ISBN-13:

- eBook: 979-8-9940365-0-1
- Paperback: 979-8-9940365-1-8
- Hardcover: 979-8-9940365-2-5

Printed in the United States of America.

First Edition

Dedication

To my husband, for your unwavering love, patience, and strength—
and to my children, for your resilience, courage, and the joy you bring to every day.

This book is for you, with all my heart.

"Love your children enough to set boundaries, even when it breaks your heart." — Unknown

Contents

Prologue —Walking into the Storm 1

Chapter 1 – Julia 4

Chapter 2 – The Walls She Built 7

Chapter 3 –Mirrors and Masks 12

Chapter 4 –Storms at Home 17

Chapter 5 –Smoke in the Room 22

Chapter 6 – The Bathroom Floor 27

Chapter 7 – The Emergency Room 33

Chapter 8 – The Transfer 37

Chapter 9 – The Breaking Point 42

Chapter 10 – The Hidden Arsenal 47

Chapter 11 – Ten Months of Storms 54

Chapter 12 – The Letter 59

Chapter 13 – A Fragile Shelter 65

Chapter 14 –Patterns and Pain: Understanding Julia . 69

Chapter 15 –Healing and Moving Forward 74

Epilogue – Life After the Storm 78

Acknowledgments 81

Resources —Support, Therapy, and Education 84

Author's Note —Guidance for Families and Caregivers
.... 90

References 92

About the Author 95

Prologue – Walking into the Storm

Julia lived on the edge of chaos, even when the world around her appeared calm. She carried a storm inside her, one no one else could see but everyone could feel. From a young age, she learned that people could not be trusted, that love could disappear without warning, and that safety was never guaranteed.

Her earliest experiences were fractured and painful. Her biological mother struggled with addiction and emotional instability, shattering Julia's sense of security before she had learned how to trust. When she was adopted by parents who loved her fiercely, she was given stability, structure, and protection. But love alone could not undo the trauma already rooted inside her.

This is a story about what it looks like to live with unhealed trauma and severe emotional dysregulation. It is the story of a child who tested boundaries, pushed people away before they could leave, and created crises that seemed to erupt without warning. It is also the story of a family's endurance, and the limits of what even the most devoted parents can fix.

Julia's journey is not simple. It is marked by danger, fear, and heartbreak. It is also a story of resilience, of hope, and of the courage required to survive, not only for the child at the center of the storm, but for the family struggling to stand beside her.

This book is not only Julia's story. It is a reflection on trauma, reactive attachment disorder, and borderline personality traits as they unfold in real life. It is an invitation to understand, to empathize, and to learn how families survive and grow when love alone is not enough.

Most importantly, it is a reminder that trauma changes lives, but it does not have to define them.

Chapter 1 – Julia

Julia sat on the edge of her bed, staring through the clear windowpane as morning light spilled across her room. Her heart pounded with a storm she could not quiet. She knew the thoughts were not rational, yet they felt undeniable. Everyone was against her. Everyone would leave. Everyone would hurt her.

In the next room, her brothers, Daniel and Leo, played noisily. They were carefree and unguarded in ways Julia both envied and resented. Their laughter tightened something in her chest. She could not tell whether it made her ache for connection or reminded her that she stood apart from it.

Julia had been adopted after early years of chaos with a biological mother who struggled with addiction and, she had been told, borderline personality disorder. She did not fully understand the diagnosis, but she understood its outcome. She learned early that love could vanish in an instant and that trust was a liability.

So, she built walls. They were high, rigid, and unyielding. She pushed people away before they could abandon her, before they could hurt her first. She loved with everything she had, or she hated with equal force. There was no middle ground. Her emotions were not simply strong. They were overwhelming, crashing over her in relentless waves that threatened to pull her under.

As her brothers' laughter drifted through the thin walls, Julia made a silent vow. She would never be vulnerable. She would never be hurt. She would fight to stay in control, even if it meant standing alone.

Chapter 2 — The Walls She Built

Julia woke to the sharp glare of morning light slicing through the cracked blinds. Her chest was already tight, as if the day had begun with a warning. Everyone will leave you. Everyone will betray you. She turned toward the empty side of her bed and felt the familiar hollow knot settle in her stomach. She was not sure who frightened her more today: the world, her parents, or herself.

From the next room came the loud, chaotic laughter of her brothers. Daniel, two years younger, never stopped moving, always teasing, always demanding attention. Leo, six years her junior, carried a fearless energy that Julia both admired and resented. Their joy sometimes felt like a reminder of everything she could not hold onto. They seemed safe in a way she had never been.

Her parents meant well. She knew that. But Julia also knew something they did not want to face:

love could disappear without warning. She had learned that lesson early, and she felt the same storms stirring inside her own heart. So, she learned to hide them. She learned to build walls.

She dressed quickly, brushing her hair until it lay perfectly in place, another layer of armor. At breakfast, her parents talked about ordinary things: school schedules, errands, plans for the weekend. Julia heard something else entirely. Criticism slipped between their words. Judgment hovered in every glance. When Daniel asked a question, it sounded mocking. When Leo spilled his juice, Julia's stomach dropped. They are going to ruin everything. Everyone will leave me.

So, she struck first.

A sharp remark to Daniel. An icy look toward Leo. Her parents exchanged tired glances, confused and frustrated. Julia barely noticed. Distance was safer than closeness. Control was safer than hope.

At school, her thoughts raced without rest. Every friendship felt temporary. Every smile carried the threat of betrayal. She swung between desperate longing for connection and sudden rejection of anyone who came too close. Teachers called her volatile. Classmates whispered that she was strange. Julia absorbed it all and filed it away under one simple truth: they do not understand me, and they never will.

Still, beneath the walls, something ached. A small, stubborn part of her wanted to trust. Wanted to be seen. Wanted to be loved without conditions. It surfaced in fleeting moments: a friend's hand on her shoulder, a teacher's quiet patience. Those moments frightened her almost as much as they comforted her. If she let herself feel them, she might be hurt. And if she were hurt, she would never forgive herself for allowing it.

By the end of the day, Julia was exhausted. Not from schoolwork, but from the constant vigilance

required to manage the emotional minefield inside her.
She slipped past her brothers when she got home and collapsed onto her bed. Her parents peeked in, offering gentle smiles. Julia returned them with careful nods, unwilling to let herself soften.

She pulled the blankets tight around her, her small fortress, and whispered a vow she had made many times before.

I will not be broken.

I will not be abandoned.

I will survive this, even if it means standing alone.

Chapter 3 – Mirrors and Masks

Julia moved through the crowded high school hallway with practiced awareness. Her backpack hung low on her shoulder, her eyes scanning groups of friends clustered in familiar patterns. She shifted herself as needed, adjusting her posture, her voice, even her expressions to match the space she entered. With each group, she became someone else. Witty and sarcastic with the theater kids. Quiet and reflective with the art students. Defiant and reckless with the skaters.

It was not about fitting in. It was about survival. Because being too much or not enough led to the same outcome. People left.

By the third period, she sat with members of the art club, describing a summer trip to Paris she had never taken. She spoke confidently about narrow streets, café tables, and museum halls. The details came easily. Her classmates leaned closer, intrigued. For a moment, she felt seen.

Then someone laughed lightly and mentioned seeing her that same summer at a local fair.

Julia froze.

A sharp panic flared in her chest. They know. They know I lied.

"That's not true," she said, keeping her voice steady despite the brittle edge beneath it. "I was in Paris."

The proof appeared almost immediately. Photos from the fair surfaced on someone's phone. The truth was undeniable. Still, Julia could not admit it. To do so would expose the fragile persona she relied on to feel worthy. If she let that collapse, what would be left? And would anyone stay?

So she doubled down.

"That's not me," she insisted. "You're mistaken."

Her friends frowned, frustration rising, but Julia barely registered their reactions. Her mind raced ahead, already bracing for abandonment. Arguing felt safer than surrender. Defending the lie felt necessary, even as it isolated her further.

After school, she walked past her brothers playing in the yard. Daniel shouted something teasing. Leo laughed. The sound pierced her, stirring resentment and longing at the same time. She wanted to join them. She wanted to belong. But belonging required vulnerability, and vulnerability always came at too high a cost.

That evening, alone in her room, Julia stood in front of the mirror. She studied her reflection, searching for something solid beneath the shifting layers. Who was she, really? The girl who traveled to Paris. The quiet artist. The sharp-tongued comedian. Or the one who trusted no one at all.

The answer slipped away each time she reached for it.

She wrapped herself in blankets and whispered into the quiet, "I am what I need to be to survive."

Her lies were not just lies. They were shields. She clung to them because believing was easier than facing the emptiness underneath. But each lie built another barrier. Each argument pushed people farther away. And with every mask she wore, Julia became more convinced that no one could ever truly see her.

So, she kept shifting. Kept performing. Kept preparing for the moment someone would finally see through her.

Because when that happened, she was certain of one thing.

The pain would be unbearable.

Chapter 4 – Storms at Home

The moment Julia walked through the front door, the familiar hum of her brothers' video game filled the living room. Daniel was stretched across the couch, controller clenched in his hands, shouting at the screen. Leo bounced beside him, fully absorbed in the chaos. Almost instantly, Julia felt panic surge through her, sharp and overwhelming. The house felt hostile. The noise felt intentional. It felt like they were turning on her.

She moved toward the television with rigid purpose. Without warning, she yanked the controller from Daniel's hands.

"Stop!" she shouted, her voice already shaking. "Stop it. You're trying to hurt me."

Daniel stared at her, startled. "What are you talking about? I'm just playing."

Leo looked up as Julia stepped directly in front of the screen, blocking it completely.

"No!" she screamed. "You both hate me. You want me gone. You want me dead."

Her words came fast and jagged, tumbling over each other as her chest heaved.

"I can feel it. You're against me. You always have been."

Daniel reached for the remote. Julia snatched it away and spun toward them, her eyes wide and frantic. "See? This is exactly what I mean. You're always trying to hurt me. You don't care about me. I can't take this anymore."

In the kitchen, her parents exchanged a quick, tense glance. Months earlier, they had installed cameras in the shared spaces, not to spy, but to protect. The goal was safety. When Julia's fear escalated into aggression, they needed a way to intervene without relying on memory or interpretation. The footage often told a calmer, clearer story than the chaos unfolding in the moment.

Julia did not see the cameras. She did not see concern or caution. She saw enemies.

Every laugh, every movement, every ordinary interaction felt like proof of betrayal. Her response came from the only place she knew: accusation, escalation, control. What began as siblings playing a game became a battlefield. The living room was filled with shouting, tears, and certainty that she was under attack.

Eventually, the storm burned itself out. Julia retreated to her room, exhausted and hollow. In the quiet that followed, she felt both triumphant and ashamed. Triumphant because she believed she had defended herself. Ashamed because something deep inside her knew she had lost control again.

When her parents tried to explain what the cameras showed, Julia could not absorb it. The truth felt unbearable. Accepting it meant admitting that her fear had misled her. That felt too close to betrayal. She argued relentlessly, her words sharp and unyielding, clinging to her version of events because it felt safer than doubt.

Beneath the fury was the same fear that had shaped her life from the beginning. Fear of being unwanted. Fear of abandonment. Fear that love could disappear without warning.

Her parents watched carefully, trying to remain calm, trying to protect all three children at once. They understood something Julia could not yet see: her storms were not just dangerous. They were desperate. Each eruption was both a threat and a plea. Push them away before they leave. Hold them close before they disappear.

Julia lived suspended between those two impulses, never able to rest in either one.

Chapter 5 – Smoke in the Room

The house was quiet. Julia's father was at work, and her mother had just stepped into the shower. Julia sat on her bed, a cigarette trembling between her fingers.

Just one, she told herself.

She flicked the lighter and inhaled, the harsh smoke curling into her lungs. It burned, but it also steadied her. For a moment, the world felt quieter.

Then the smell reached the bathroom.

Her mother's eyes flew open. Shampoo still clinging to her hair, she rushed from the shower and wrapped a towel around herself, her heart already pounding. Smoke. She knew that smell. Instinct took over.

Julia's bedroom door was closed, but the scent was unmistakable. Her mother knocked once, gently. "Julia?" she called.

No answer.

She opened the door a crack, and the smoke confirmed what she already knew.

"Did you," she began, then stopped.

Julia's eyes met hers, wide and defiant. "No. I didn't smoke anything."

Her voice cracked, caught between anger and panic.

"I can smell it," her mother said evenly. "Julia."

"I didn't," Julia insisted, breath coming fast. "I swear. I just lit a piece of paper on fire."

The words faltered as she repeated them, trying to convince both of them.

Her mother knew better. But she also knew confrontation, here and now, would only ignite another storm. She took a slow breath and stepped back. "Come sit with me," she said. "Please."

Julia stumbled into the living room and collapsed onto the couch, tears pouring freely. "I didn't smoke. I swear. Why won't you believe me?

Why do you hate me?" Her words tumbled out in sobs. "I can't tell you the truth because then you'll think I smoked."

Her mother sat beside her, steady and quiet. She did not argue. She did not punish. She did not escalate. Time stretched. Julia repeated herself again and again, desperate for belief, desperate for relief, while her mother stayed grounded, anchoring the room with her presence.

Finally, she spoke.

"Julia," she said softly. "If you bring me the cigarette and the lighter, I won't think you smoked."

Julia froze.

"Are you sure?"

"I just need to know you're safe," her mother said. "That's all."

After a long pause, Julia jumped up. Seconds later, she returned, holding the cigarette and lighter in shaking hands. She sat back down, still crying, still raw, but the tightness in her chest eased just enough to breathe.

Her mother reached out and brushed a strand of damp hair from Julia's face. Nothing more needed to be said.

For that moment, Julia felt safe. She felt loved. The world did not feel entirely against her.

It was only one day in the life of a teenager living with severe emotional dysregulation. A day filled with fear, denial, and overwhelming intensity. But it was also proof that patience, clarity, and restraint could meet the storm, even if only briefly.

Chapter 6 — The Bathroom Floor

The next morning, Julia walked through the school hallways with a hollow, buzzing sensation under her skin. The night before clung to her thoughts like smoke. Shame. Defensiveness. The fear of being caught. The fear of losing control. Her emotions felt stretched thin, barely contained.

By mid-morning, the pressure inside her became unbearable. Small things cut deeply. A teacher's impatient look. A friend laughing with someone else. Each moment landed like a personal rejection. Her chest tightened until she thought she might burst.

She slipped out of class and walked quickly to the girls' bathroom at the end of the hallway, the one with the flickering light and chipped tiles where few students went. She locked herself into the far stall. Her hands shook.

She needed relief. Something immediate. Something she could feel.

From behind the sanitary napkin dispenser, she pulled out a razor blade she had hidden weeks earlier. Her breath hitched. She pressed the metal against her skin and drew it across her wrist. The sting came first, then warmth, then release. For one brief moment, the noise inside her head softened.

The stall door creaked.

"Julia?"

Serena, a girl from her class, stood frozen just inside the bathroom. Her eyes dropped to Julia's wrist. The color drained from her face. She swayed once, then collapsed to the floor.

Julia stared, her mind snapping from relief to terror. Not because of the blood, but because she had been seen. The fear hit instantly and completely. Now they know. Now everyone will know. Now they'll leave.

Another student entered seconds later, gasped, and ran for help.

Within minutes, the principal, Mrs. Harland, and the guidance counselor, Ms. Reyes, rushed into the bathroom. Serena was revived and escorted out, shaken and pale. Julia remained seated against the stall wall, gripping her arm, her expression flickering between panic and defiance.

"Julia, can you tell us what happened?" Mrs. Harland asked quietly.

Julia stared straight ahead. "I slipped. I fell against something sharp."

Ms. Reyes crouched beside her. "Julia, there are multiple cuts. This doesn't look accidental."

"It was an accident," Julia snapped, her voice cracking. "You don't understand."

Mrs. Harland and Ms. Reyes exchanged a brief glance. They stood close together, listening carefully.

"Tell me again what happened," Ms. Reyes said gently.

Julia's eyes darted. "I was cleaning something. It broke. I tried to pick it up and it cut me."

Mrs. Harland tilted her head slightly. "That isn't what you said earlier."

"I did say that," Julia insisted.

"You told me you fell," the principal replied evenly.

Julia froze.

The silence that followed felt unbearable. Both women waited, calm and patient, which somehow made everything worse.

"You're twisting my words," Julia shouted. "Why are you doing this? Why do you hate me?"

"Julia, we're not trying to trap you," Ms. Reyes said. "We're trying to help."

"No, you're not," Julia screamed, tears spilling over. "You're both against me. You're lying. I didn't do anything wrong."

Her emotions erupted all at once. Fear, rage, shame, confusion collided inside her, spilling outward. She paced in tight circles, clutching her wrist, unable to tolerate the pressure of being questioned. She could not tell the truth. She could not allow herself to be seen.

To tell one consistent story meant choosing vulnerability. Vulnerability felt dangerous. Vulnerability felt like annihilation.

Mrs. Harland stepped back to give her space. Ms. Reyes spoke softly. "We need the truth so we can keep you safe."

Julia slid down the wall and sobbed, overwhelmed and wordless. She could not respond. She was trapped between the terror of being exposed and the terror of being abandoned.

This was not an isolated incident. It was another day shaped by emotional dysregulation so intense that pain had to be pulled outward to be survived. A day where even help felt like a threat.

Chapter 7 – The Emergency Room

The call from the school came in the middle of the day. Julia's father listened quietly as the principal explained. The cut. The fainting student. The conflicting accounts. He did not interrupt. When the call ended, he left immediately, driving first to the school and then straight to the hospital.

The family had moved only months earlier, three hours away from everything familiar, so the mother could accept a new position with the school district. The transition had been difficult for everyone, but especially for Julia.

He stayed with her through triage, through the nurse's questions, through the first set of vitals. He watched her emotions shift with ease. Fear softened into sadness. Sadness turned into relief. Each expression appeared and disappeared smoothly, like a series of practiced masks.

When he had to leave for his second shift job, he called his wife and asked her to come.

By the time the mother arrived, the hospital hallway felt unnaturally bright and quiet. She paused before entering the room, bracing herself.

Julia sat upright in the bed, her wrist neatly bandaged. She looked calm. Almost pleased. When her mother stepped inside, Julia tilted her head and asked softly, a hint of amusement in her voice,

"Did I embarrass you?"

Her mother took a breath. "Was that your intention?"

Julia didn't answer with words. She smiled. It was not an apologetic smile. Not an ashamed one. It was familiar. A smile edged with satisfaction.

Julia loved hospitals.

She loved the structure. The attention. The way each nurse arrived without history, unaware of yesterday's outburst or last week's crisis. In the hospital, she could begin again. She could become whoever she needed to be.

And the staff believed her. Her tears came easily. Her voice trembled at the right moments. She spoke quietly about feeling unsafe at home. About being misunderstood. About feeling alone. Notes were taken. Reassurances offered. She was told she was brave.

Julia absorbed it all. The validation. The sympathy. The way adults leaned closer when she spoke.

For her, the hospital was not frightening. It was relieving. It was freedom from consequence. It was a stage.

And tonight, she was at the center of it.

Chapter 8 – The Transfer

When the crisis worker arrived, Julia shifted again. This time, she became colder, sharper, and more deliberate. She told the worker she intended to kill herself. Her voice was steady. Her expression was unreadable. There was no hesitation in the response. The protocol was clear.

Within hours, a sheriff escorted Julia from the small emergency room to a psychiatric facility two counties away.

Her mother watched as her daughter was led down the hallway, hands clasped in front of her, the deputy following a step behind. The scene felt surreal, jarring, and yet disturbingly familiar. Julia had been unraveling for months, slipping further into behaviors the family did not understand and could not stop.

At the facility, Julia found new listeners. Nurses. Technicians. Therapists. None of them knew her history. None of them knew her patterns.

She began to tell her story.

She said her mother had threatened to kill her. She said her brothers wished she were dead. She presented herself as frightened, fragile, and in need of rescue. The words came easily, delivered with conviction and emotion.

But the stories were not the end of it.

Julia made threats. Specific ones. Directed at her mother and her younger brothers. The staff documented everything. Child and Youth Services was notified. An investigation was opened.

For weeks, the family lived in a constant state of dread. Investigators interviewed them, reviewed timelines, and examined statements. Every phone call tightened the knot in their stomachs.

When the report was finally released, it confirmed what the parents had known all along. Julia was not the victim in need of protection. She was the one posing a danger to her underage siblings.

She remained hospitalized for ten days.

Before discharge, the staff handed the parents a list. It was long, typed, formal, and uncompromising. These were not recommendations. They were conditions.

All sharp objects had to be removed or locked away.

All medications, including vitamins, had to be secured.

Weapons of any kind were to be inaccessible.

Julia had to be visually checked every fifteen minutes.

She could not be left alone, ever.

She had to take three medications, each swallowed under direct supervision, followed by food to ensure nothing was hidden.

The staff reviewed the instructions carefully. Then, reviewed them again.

This was not a plan for healing. It was a manual for survival.

On the drive home, the mother folded the paper and placed it in her bag. She stared out the window at the darkening sky, feeling the weight of it settle deep inside her.

Julia was coming home.

But home would never be the same.

Chapter 9 – The Breaking Point

For two weeks after Julia returned, the family lived in constant vigilance. Every sound felt sharp. Every hour was tense. They followed every instruction exactly. Knives locked away. Medications secured. Checks every fifteen minutes, day and night. One parent was always awake. One was always listening.

Still, the house did not feel safe.

Julia drifted further from reality. At times, she spoke as if she were living in another world, responding to questions no one had asked, describing events that had never occurred. She paced endlessly. She argued with unseen people. Her siblings stayed close to their mother or disappeared into quiet rooms. The parents avoided sudden movements and raised voices. They lived cautiously, like intruders in their own home, measuring each moment by whether it could provoke the next crisis.

Then one night, it did.

Julia stepped out of her bedroom, pale and shaking, her hand pressed tightly against her thigh.

"Mom," she said softly. "I can't make it stop."

Her mother saw the blood immediately. Instinct took over. She called for her husband, grabbed the nearest clean clothing, and wrapped it tightly around Julia's leg to slow the bleeding. Julia swayed, detached, as if watching from somewhere far away.

Her father carried her to the car and drove to the hospital, again. His hands trembled on the steering wheel. The mother stayed behind just long enough to call the emergency room and tell them they were coming.

The nurse who answered spoke with calm certainty.

"We'll take care of her," she said. "You're not alone. She'll be safe here. And you will get through this."

Before ending the call, the nurse offered a quiet prayer. It was unexpected. It was the first time in weeks the mother felt herself breathe.

Julia was admitted that night. The doctors and mental health staff reviewed her history, assessed her condition, and reached the same conclusion.

She needed long-term care.

Not days. Not weeks. A year.

There was no dramatic goodbye. No final conversation. The staff explained that contact would interfere with treatment. Julia needed distance, structure, and safety.

The parents went home without her.

They cried in the car. They cried in the kitchen. They cried in the quiet spaces she had once filled with noise, conflict, and relentless emotion.

She was gone, but she did not leave them.

They carried her with them every day. Her laughter. Her fury. Her fear. Her brilliance. Her pain.

The house felt hollow in ways they could not name.

Chapter 10 – The Hidden Arsenal

The house was finally quiet the night Julia left for the hospital, the last night she would ever sleep under their roof. The boys were in bed. Her husband sat silently at the kitchen table, staring at nothing. The mother walked down the hallway toward Julia's room, intending only to gather the few items the hospital had requested.

When she opened the bedroom door, the air felt wrong. Heavy. Still. She paused, staring at the rumpled blankets, the piles of clothes, the corner where Julia used to curl up when she said she "couldn't breathe." Something inside her whispered, *Look deeper.*

She did not yet know that what she was about to uncover would change everything they believed about what had been happening inside their home.

She began with Julia's dresser. On top lay neatly folded panty liners, far more than necessary. When she picked one up, something about the weight felt off. She peeled back the adhesive strip and froze.

Pressed carefully between layers of cotton was a razor blade.

Her breath caught. She checked another. Then another. Each one concealed with clinical precision, as if Julia had been preparing for a future no one else could see.

A chill moved through her. How long had these been hidden? How close had the boys come to finding them? How many meals had they shared, unaware that danger sat just a room away?

Then she noticed the tampons.

At first, they looked ordinary, wrapped, and unused. But when she lifted one, the weight shifted wrong in her hand. She opened it carefully.

Taped to the cardboard applicator was a sewing needle.

Another held a sharpened pin.

Another, a small shard of razor.

The realization landed hard. Julia had not only been hiding tools, but also engineering them.

Her room was not simply cluttered or chaotic. It was deliberate. A workshop. An armory. A lifeline to pain, or perhaps the only way she knew to survive the storm inside her mind.

On the nightstand sat what looked like a wadded napkin, slightly damp. When the mother unfolded it, tiny beads of partially dissolved pills clung to the fibers, medication Julia was supposed to take, medication she had pretended to swallow.

Behind the desk sat a small beverage cooler. When the mother opened it, she gagged. Inside were vomited pills, layered, collected, and preserved. A quiet record of every dose Julia had refused to let enter her body.

Then she found the retainer case. The retainer inside had been broken into jagged, weapon-like pieces.

Even the most ordinary object had been transformed into something sharp, something dangerous.

She kept searching.

Paper clips filed down to points.

Metal rings torn from notebooks.

Broken plastic from DVD cases, sharpened like crude knives.

A piece of glass wrapped in tissue, hidden inside a pillowcase. Another pressed into the corner of the mattress.

Objects taped to the underside of dresser drawers, plastic picks, sharpened pencils, and more fragments of glass.

Every hiding place was intentional. Logical. Methodical.

This was not impulsive behavior.

This was preparation.

The last thing she checked was Julia's makeup bag. Tucked between brushes and mascara tubes, wrapped in cosmetic wipes, were piercing needles, thin, long, and lethal.

Her stomach turned.

This was not teenage rebellion.

This was not moodiness or attention-seeking.

This was a child fighting a war no one could see, arming herself with anything she could find.

The mother sank to the floor, surrounded by objects that could have killed her daughter or someone else. The weight of it pressed down until she could barely breathe.

For years, they had believed they were keeping Julia safe.

They locked away knives.

They secured medications.

They searched her room.

They set boundaries.

They watched.

They hoped.

They prayed.

They tried.

And still, Julia had outmaneuvered every safeguard.

She had hidden blades where no one would think to look.

She had created danger from the ordinary.

She had lived inside a world they could not reach.

Sitting there, surrounded by the artifacts of her daughter's pain, the mother finally understood:

Julia had been drowning for a long time before anyone realized she was underwater.

Chapter 11 – Ten Months of Storms

The first weeks inside the facility were chaotic, almost familiar in their intensity. Julia tested every boundary, challenged every rule, and pushed against every authority figure she encountered. She ran repeatedly. Each time, state police were called to retrieve her and bring her back.

Once, she was found inside a stranger's home, convinced it belonged to her simply because it "looked nice." Staff escorted her out, restrained her when necessary, and returned her to the unit. Again.

She fought with other patients. She shouted at the staff. She entered restricted areas without permission, not out of confusion but defiance. The rules themselves felt like an insult to her autonomy.

Family therapy sessions were held weekly. Her parents attended every one, hopeful but cautious. At first, Julia sat silently. Then she began redirecting every conversation toward blame. Nothing was ever her responsibility. Every conflict, every consequence, every broken rule belonged to someone else.

Her stories shifted depending on who was listening. Claims of sexual abuse at fourteen. Being raped. Still being a virgin. Abuse by a boyfriend. Identifying as a lesbian. Each version contradicted the last. When confronted with inconsistencies or facts, she shut down, walked out, or erupted into hysteria. Reality was negotiable. Accountability was not.

The staff tried everything they could offer. Structured therapies. Group work. Independent living skills. Each program was designed to prepare her for stability beyond the facility. Julia refused them all. She rejected guidance, resisted support, and declined participation in anything that required reflection or responsibility.

She told everyone she would leave as soon as she turned eighteen. She wanted freedom. No rules. No oversight. No limits. What she wanted was autonomy without accountability.

Her family remained firm. She could only return home if she could be safe, and if her younger brothers could be safe. Julia did not accept this. She triangulated constantly, attempting to turn staff against her parents, siblings against one another, and anyone willing to listen into an ally. Her narratives were strategic, designed to isolate, divide, and control.

When her eighteenth birthday arrived, she did not leave. She stayed.

Four more months passed. She continued refusing treatment until insurance coverage ended. Without participation or progress, the facility could no longer justify her stay.

On her eighteenth birthday, Julia legally severed all ties with her adoptive parents.

No contact. No accountability. No reconciliation.

She eventually left the facility to live with her biological mother. The family she had lived with for nearly two decades, the family that had fought to protect her and keep everyone safe, was gone from her life.

The ten months inside the facility were not healing. They were containment. A storm held within walls. Julia remained untethered, unwilling to accept limits, reality, or responsibility. For her, freedom meant walking away from those who loved her and stepping into the world on her own terms.

Chapter 12 – The Letter

The months that followed were quiet in ways the family had forgotten were possible. The house felt calmer, lighter. And yet the grief settled heavily in every room.

The parents and the boys entered therapy, trying to understand how to rebuild after years of living on emotional fault lines. They spoke often about boundaries, safety, responsibility, and love. Not the sentimental kind. The hard kind. The kind that requires distance when closeness becomes dangerous.

Over time, one truth became impossible to avoid.

Loving Julia did not make her safe. Loving her did not mean allowing her behavior to continue destroying them.

And so, they wrote a letter.

Not in anger.

Not in punishment.

But in truth.

They wrote it together carefully. When they finished, they knew it was the hardest thing they had ever put into words.

Dear Julia,

Because of your original hurt and trauma, you have been acting and reacting in unhealthy ways. Trauma is not just something that happens to you. It happens inside you. What we do not work through, we act out, often in dangerous and destructive ways.

There is something deeper happening in your thinking and processing. You continue to hurt us and those around you through your choices. It is painful to watch you move further into behaviors that place you and others at risk. Your choices belong to you, but their consequences fall on everyone who loves you.

We are heartbroken because we did not cause this, we cannot control it, and we cannot fix it. Only you can choose to face your trauma and do the work required to heal. You were given a real opportunity to receive help, and you chose not to participate.

We must face reality. Our relationship with you has become emotionally destructive. You repeatedly tear our family down and prevent any of us from growing. We set expectations that were realistic and clear. You refuse to acknowledge your behavior, take responsibility, or recognize the harm caused.

Our family could not function with you in it. We lived in constant crisis management, afraid of what might happen next. You could be kind and engaging when things went your way, but when you felt upset, jealous, or denied, you controlled us through threats, outbursts, and a lack of impulse control.

Trust cannot survive constant violation. We cannot enable destructive behavior and call it love.

Lies, theft, threats, and manipulation became patterns. When truth is distorted to avoid responsibility, relationships become unsafe.

Our boundaries are simple. You must be safe, and you must treat us safely and respectfully. Until you are willing to take responsibility, seek help, and respect those boundaries, we must restrict the emotional access you have to us.

These boundaries are not meant to fix you. They exist to protect what remains healthy in our lives.

We are focusing on healing and rebuilding. We love you deeply. That is why this hurts so much. We are grieving a relationship that is no longer sustainable.

This goodbye may be temporary, or it may last years. That depends on you.

We hope you choose healing. We hope you find safety, stability, and peace. You are an adult now, and your choices will shape the life you build.

May God watch over you and protect you.

With love,

Mom, Dad, Daniel, and Leo

They did not read the letter aloud. They placed it in an envelope and set it aside.

The mother cried for a long time.

The father went outside and fixed something that was not broken.

The boys sat together on the couch, leaning against one another in rare stillness.

It was not just a letter.

It was an ending they never wanted.

And the beginning of learning how to breathe again.

Chapter 13 – A Fragile Shelter

Julia lived with her biological mother for three months.

On paper, she was enrolled to complete her senior year of high school. In reality, the days dissolved into missed classes, skipped obligations, and no routine at all. Absences accumulated until the school removed her from the roster entirely.

Drugs entered her daily life. Shoplifting and theft followed. Threats made at school drew the attention of authorities once again, resulting in another placement. This one was short-term, rigid, and focused on containment rather than treatment.

Her biological mother attempted to impose structure. She pursued child support from the adoptive parents. She set boundaries. Chores. Shared responsibilities. Basic expectations for safety and respect.

Julia resisted everyone.

She stole when she could. She manipulated when confronted. She left whenever rules were enforced. Every step toward accountability was met with defiance. Every attempt at connection was twisted into control.

The biological mother's resolve eroded quickly. She tried consequences. She tried guidance. She tried holding firm. But Julia's behavior was relentless.

Before her biological mother could abandon her again, Julia left.

Three months. Three months of chaos, theft, threats, and manipulation. And once again, she walked away, leaving confusion and grief behind her.

The pattern was unmistakable. No home, no caregiver, no set of rules altered the outcome. Julia's search for control, fueled by unhealed trauma, continued without restraint.

And once again, the adults who loved her were left behind, trying to understand how love could coexist with so much damage, and why nothing ever seemed to reach her.

Chapter 14 – Patterns and Pain: Understanding Julia

Julia's story is not only one of chaos, rebellion, and heartbreak. It is also a study in how early trauma can shape development, how unhealed wounds can distort perception, and how survival patterns learned in childhood can persist into adulthood. Understanding Julia does not excuse her behavior. It allows it to be placed in context.

Trauma is not limited to a single event. It is an experience that becomes embedded in the brain and body. Julia's earliest years were marked by instability, disrupted caregiving, and exposure to substance use. Her biological mother struggled with addiction and significant emotional dysregulation. Julia's earliest attachments were fractured before trust could fully form.

Trauma does not simply happen to a person. It alters the nervous system, emotional regulation, and sense of safety. Unhealed trauma often manifests as hypervigilance, intense fear of abandonment, distrust, and an ongoing need to control one's environment. Julia's running away, lying, boundary testing, and manipulation were not random. They were maladaptive attempts to manage internal chaos and restore a sense of control.

Julia's relational patterns reflected behaviors commonly observed in individuals with significant attachment disruption. She struggled to form secure bonds, even with caregivers who were consistent, protective, and emotionally invested. Although her adoptive parents provided structure and care, Julia's internalized fear of rejection led her to repeatedly push them away.

When attachment feels unsafe, vulnerability can register as danger. In these circumstances, behaviors such as lying, stealing, aggression, or triangulation often emerge as protective strategies rather than intentional cruelty. Julia's attempts to control relationships were rooted in fear, not malice, even when the impact was deeply harmful.

As Julia entered adolescence, her behavior increasingly aligned with traits commonly associated with borderline personality disorder. These traits included: intense fear of abandonment, all-or-nothing thinking, unstable self-image and shifting identity, impulsivity and risk-taking, and severe emotional dysregulation.

These traits are not character flaws. They reflect profound difficulty regulating emotion, maintaining relational stability, and tolerating distress. Julia's intensity and volatility were expressions of pain she lacked the tools to manage.

Across settings, Julia's behavior followed a consistent pattern: internal distress escalated, she acted out to relieve or control that distress, and a crisis occurred.

An external intervention followed, and temporary stabilization occurred. The cycle resumed.

This pattern repeated in homes, schools, and treatment facilities because the underlying trauma and attachment disruptions remained unresolved.

A trauma-informed understanding is essential for families and professionals working with individuals who experience severe emotional dysregulation.

Boundaries are protective, not punitive. Behavior is communication, even when it is dangerous. Healing requires long-term, specialized intervention. Love without limits can become enabling.

Julia's story illustrates the immense strain placed on families who love deeply while navigating unsafe behaviors. It also underscores a difficult truth: compassion and accountability must coexist. Safety must come first.

Chapter 15 – Healing and Moving Forward

The house is quieter now. The constant vigilance, the anticipation of crisis, and the feeling of living on edge have faded. Julia is gone. The grief remains, but so does relief.

For the parents, healing does not mean forgetting. It has meant reclaiming safety. They spent years managing crises no family should face alone. They sought professional guidance, implemented boundaries, and made decisions rooted in protection rather than fear. In doing so, they restored stability for the children who remained.

Daniel and Leo have begun to heal in visible ways. They play freely. They argue without escalation. They express emotion without fear of explosive consequences. They are learning that home can be predictable, that love can be steady, and that boundaries are not punishments.

The parents have come to accept a painful truth: they did not cause Julia's trauma, and they could not undo it. Accepting this allowed them to release responsibility for outcomes they could not control and focus instead on what they could protect.

For families navigating similar realities, it is vital to know that support exists. Trauma-informed care and clinicians experienced with personality disorders are essential. Healing is not quick, and it is not linear. But safety, peace, and hope are possible.

Healing requires boundaries.

Healing requires support.

Healing sometimes requires distance.

The family now measures progress in quiet moments: shared meals, unguarded laughter, and nights without fear. Trauma leaves scars, but it does not have to dictate the future.

They look at their sons and see resilience. They see possibilities. They see lives no longer defined by chaos.

After the storm, they have learned how to stand in the light.

Epilogue – Life After the Storm

Julia's story is unfinished. It continues beyond these pages, shaped by her choices and the paths she takes. This book does not claim to predict her future. It tells the truth about the past.

For her adoptive family, survival required honesty, boundaries, and courage. They learned that love does not mean tolerating harm. They learned that protection is not abandonment. They learned that some storms cannot be calmed from the inside.

Daniel and Leo are growing up in a home defined by safety rather than fear. The parents continue their own healing, carrying both grief and hope forward together.

For those walking similar paths, the message is clear: seek help early, prioritize safety, and trust that choosing boundaries is not a failure of love.

Trauma alters lives. But it does not erase the possibility of healing. Even after the darkest storms, life can be rebuilt.

Acknowledgments

This book would not exist without the strength, support, and love of the people who walked beside us through one of the most difficult journeys a family can face.

To my husband, your steadiness, compassion, and unwavering belief in our family carried us when the weight felt too heavy. Thank you for being my partner in every sense of the word.

To my children, each of you has shaped my heart in ways I never anticipated. Thank you for your patience, your honesty, and your courage as we navigated circumstances far beyond what any child should have to witness or understand. You are my greatest teachers.

To the professionals who stood with us, therapists, social workers, case managers, and medical teams, thank you for your expertise, your guidance, and for helping us see a path forward when we couldn't find one ourselves.

To the friends and family members who showed up quietly and consistently, with meals, phone calls, rides, or simply a listening ear, your presence mattered more than you know.

To the countless parents, caregivers, and adoptive families who are fighting similar battles: your resilience inspired me to write this book. You are not alone.

And finally, to the child at the center of this story, thank you for the lessons, the challenges, and the reminders of how complex, fragile, and fierce the human heart can be. Your journey has shaped all of us, and we continue to hope for your healing and peace.

Resources — Support, Therapy, and Education

Therapy and Mental Health Support

- **National Education Alliance for BPD (NEABPD)** –

  https://www.borderlinepersonalitydisorder.org

  Provides information, webinars, and resources for families, educators, and individuals affected by BPD.

- **National Alliance on Mental Illness (NAMI)** –

  https://www.nami.org

  Offers free support groups, educational resources, and guidance for families of individuals with mental health conditions.

- **Psychology Today Therapist Directory** –

  https://www.psychologytoday.com/us/therapists

  Find licensed therapists specializing in trauma, BPD, and attachment disorders in your area.

- **Dialectical Behavior Therapy (DBT) Resources**
    - *DBT Skills Training Manual* by Marsha M. Linehan
    - DBT-focused therapy can help individuals with BPD learn emotional regulation, interpersonal effectiveness, and distress tolerance.
- **Trauma-Informed Therapy**
    Therapists trained in trauma-focused cognitive behavioral therapy (TF-CBT), Eye Movement Desensitization and Reprocessing (EMDR), or other trauma-informed approaches can help survivors process and heal.

Parenting and Family Support

- **Tara Brach, PhD** – https://www.tarabrach.com
    Offers guidance on mindfulness, self-

compassion, and emotional regulation, useful for parents coping with stress.

- **National Child Traumatic Stress Network (NCTSN)** – https://www.nctsn.org
Provides resources for parents and caregivers on understanding and supporting children with trauma histories.

- **"Stop Walking on Eggshells" by Paul T. Mason & Randi Kreger**
A practical guide for family members of individuals with BPD.

- **Support Groups for Families of BPD or Trauma-Affected Children**
Many local hospitals, mental health clinics, and nonprofit organizations offer peer-led support groups. Search for local BPD family support or caregiver support groups.

Educational Resources

- **Books on BPD and Trauma**

    - *I Hate You—Don't Leave Me* by Jerold J. Kreisman & Hal Straus
    - *The Essential Family Guide to Borderline Personality Disorder* by Randi Kreger
    - *Understanding the Borderline Mother* by Christine Ann Lawson

- **Online Articles and Webinars**

    - NEABPD webinars for families and caregivers
    - NAMI online guides and articles on personality disorders and trauma

Crisis Resources

- **988 Suicide & Crisis Lifeline (U.S.)** – Dial 988 Immediate support for anyone in emotional distress or crisis.

- **Crisis Text Line** – Text **HELLO** to 741741

  Free, confidential support via text for those experiencing a crisis.

- **Local Emergency Services**

  Always call 911 in the U.S. if there is an immediate risk of harm to self or others.

Note to readers:

Caring for someone with unhealed trauma, emotional dysregulation, or BPD can be overwhelming. Professional guidance is essential, and you are not alone. Support is available, and seeking help is an act of courage—for yourself and those you love.

Author's Note — Guidance for Families and Caregivers

If you find yourself reading this book because someone you love is struggling with trauma, emotional dysregulation, or Borderline Personality Disorder (BPD), know that you are not alone. These situations are challenging, exhausting, and often heartbreaking—but support exists. Seeking help from a therapist who specializes in trauma and BPD is essential. Professional guidance can help you establish boundaries, protect your well-being, and navigate the complexities of these relationships.

It is important to remember that loving someone does not mean enabling behaviors that are unsafe or destructive. Healing is a long process, for both the person struggling and the family around them. Set boundaries, seek support, and focus on safety—both emotional and physical—for yourself and those you care for.

References

Bath, H., & Seita, J. (2018). *The three pillars of transforming care: Trauma and resilience in the other 23 hours.* The Association of Children's Residential & Community Services.

Brisch, K. H. (2012). *Treating attachment disorders: From theory to therapy* (2nd ed.). Guilford Press.

Ford, J. D., & Courtois, C. A. (Eds.). (2013). *Treating complex traumatic stress disorders in children and adolescents: Scientific foundations and therapeutic models.* Guilford Press.

Hughes, D. A. (2017). *Building the bonds of attachment: Awakening love in deeply troubled children* (3rd ed.). Rowman & Littlefield.

Kreger, R., & Mason, P. T. (2020). *Stop walking on eggshells: Taking your life back when someone you care about has borderline personality disorder* (3rd ed.). New Harbinger Publications.

Kreger, R., & Mason, P. T. (2020). *Stop walking on eggshells for parents: How to help your child regulate emotions, maintain boundaries, and build mental fitness.* New Harbinger Publications.

Linehan, M. M. (2015). *DBT skills training manual* (2nd ed.). Guilford Press.

Perry, B. D., & Szalavitz, M. (2021). *What happened to you? Conversations on trauma, resilience, and healing.* Mariner Books.

TerKeurst, L. (2022). *Good boundaries and goodbyes: Loving others without losing the best of who you are.* Thomas Nelson.

Van der Kolk, B. A. (2014). *The body keeps the score: Brain, mind, and body in the healing of trauma.* Viking.

About the Author

RJ Koehler is an educator, mother, advocate, and writer living in Northern Pennsylvania. She is the proud parent of many children—each one a unique gift in her life—and she loves them all deeply and unconditionally.

Through her experiences raising and working with children with complex emotional and behavioral needs, she has gained a deep understanding of trauma, attachment, and the challenges families face when navigating mental health crises. Her writing combines honesty, empathy, and insight, offering readers a window into the realities of raising children with intense emotional needs while balancing love, boundaries, and hope.

RJ Koehler's work aims to educate, encourage, and provide guidance to parents, caregivers, and families who may be facing similar challenges, showing that even in the most difficult circumstances, resilience and healing are possible.

www.ingramcontent.com/pod-product-compliance
Lightning Source LLC
Chambersburg PA
CBHW050916160426
43194CB00011B/2425